RIVERS OF JOY

RIVERS OF JOY

A Celebration of Water.

The Paintings of Shirley Deterding.
Text by John Bailey.

CREEL
PUBLISHING

First published in Great Britain by Creel Publishing, Norfolk. 1992

© Shirley Deterding and John Bailey 1992

Shirley Deterding has for many years painted under the name of Shirley Carnt.

British Library Cataloguing-in-Publication Data:
A catalogue record for this book is available from the British Library.

ISBN 0 873944 02 0

Designed and Typeset by Harper Lapping, Hethersett, Norfolk. (0603) 812522
Printed in Great Britain by the Bath Press.

For further copies of this book and other titles available, contact
Creel Publishing, 20 High Street, Cawston, Norfolk NR10 4AA.

Dust jacket, front cover illustration: Michael's River, Labrador.

Dust jacket, back cover illustration: River Thurne, Norfolk.

Contents

Page 7   Foreword by Hugh Falkus

Page 8   Introduction: Water Passion

Page 12   The Distant Cast

Page 14   The Redds

Page 16   View From A Bridge

Page 18   The Painting Lady of Glencoe

Page 20   Yards of Silver

Page 22   The Bittern's World

Page 24   The Monster

Page 30   Forgotten River

Page 32   The Last Burbot

Page 34   Impossible Rivers

Page 36   Colours of Spring

Page 38   The Wormer

Page 40   Bothy Life

Page 44   The Buddha

Page 48   The Cry of the Loon

Page 50   For the Love of Salmon

Page 56   The Back Cast

Page 58   Out of Constable

Page 60   Michael's River

Page 62   Ferox!

Page 66   Estate Lakes

Page 68   An Angler Remembers

Page 72   The Magic of the Findhorn

Page 76   The Frozen Marsh

Page 78   The Explorer

Page 80   Blind As An Eagle

Page 82   The Leaper

Page 84   Celtic Pike

Page 86   Questions of Silver

Page 90   A Norfolk Scene

Page 92   The Creek

Page 95   Appendix

To our partners Jimmy and Joy,

who have invested so much in time, patience, support and encouragement.

Our deepest thanks.

Foreword by Hugh Falkus.

This is by no means another book of parrotted advice on tackle, tactics and technique. Its horizon extends to more important objectives than the mere catching of fish.

I have known Shirley Deterding for very many years and am well aware of her profound feeling for the countryside and everything within it: a quality reflected in her beautiful paintings of landscapes and rivers I know so well. From both his writing and the time we have spent talking together, I know that John Bailey shares the same deep passion for policies of sensible conservation. And it is this central theme that has prompted their collaboration in a book which is not only in lavish praise of our beautiful waters and the all-too-precious fish that haunt them, but an indictment of the forces that threaten their destruction.

Shirley Deterding and John Bailey are neither fools nor dreamers. Echoing throughout their book is the clarion call of warning. Untended, things simply will not stay as they are much longer in our 'green and pleasant land'.

Clean, unpolluted water is the lifeblood of the countryside. Without it, everything in a landscape will wither. If we wish to retain anything of our country's natural splendour - and thankfully much of it still remains - we must be more positive in our thinking and work unremittingly to persuade our governments to prevent an environmental landslide into disaster.

This is an important book which demands to be read. A timely reminder of what must be done if, in the lifetimes of our children and grandchildren, the Rivers of Joy are not to be turned into Rivers of Despair.

Hugh Falkus
Cragg Cottage
1992

Introduction: Water Passion

From the clouds falls rain; into streams, to rivers, to reservoirs; to taps, to kettles to cups; to the bowels, to drains, to the sea and back to the clouds. Water is the essential element and is without us and within us; 70% of our brain is water, 75% of our muscles, 83% of our kidneys and 72% of our blood.

Just as powerful is our spiritual dependency on water. The waterside has long been the place for prayer, a home for the gods and the nymphs, a place of mysteries. Water is a constant marvel, whipped by the wind, ringed by the rain, darkened by storm, pearly at dawn and molten as the sun sets. Water changes its voice as often as it does its face, chattering and laughing in the sunshine and roaring to autumn storms. Only in a lake is it quiet and then after darkness when the day's breeze is off its brow.

My passion for water burst upon me when I was four by a Welsh river. It was clear, fast and glittering under a July sky and it held a sea trout, observed day after day. To lift the veil between us and merge with its stardust form became an obsession and when, finally, a late night angler deceived the fish and lay it on a silver tray the river lost its soul for me that summer.

So, too young yet to lift a rod, did I realise that water was my special element. Angling became the key to all manner of 'aquamagic' and a fixed point in a changing world. Still or running water, big fish or little fish, game or coarse, in hills or lowlands, nothing has mattered a damn if a rod has been in my hand. Each experience was so magical that I was soon driven to explain my passion in some way. Aged twelve, I wrote my first articles, huddled in the back of the maths room, lost in the shadows of my mind, seeing the red float go down into the dirty canal that crept its way past the leering mills and scowling hills. I failed every maths exam I ever took but I discovered a world that has grown more and more precious.

Shirley Deterding is a multi-talented woman. She is a highly respected game shooter, stalker, wildfowler, gundog breeder, photographer, writer, yachtswoman, rider, scuba-diver, skier, motor racer, fox hunter and explorer. Above all these things, though, she is a woman of water. Fishing with her too is a passion and in her case it has driven her to paint. Shirley's stream of artistry is something quite compulsive. A typical day in the highlands will see her awake before dawn, away from the lodge with dogs, easels and brushes, to paint undisturbed in the fresh light for two or three hours. Then it will be breakfast and planning the day with her guests.

Throughout, you will see her on a river bank, in a boat, half way up a corrie, sketching a scene, noting down colours or completing a painting despite the drizzle, the midges or a wind gusting to gale. Then Shirley is an extraordinary woman and hardly one to be dismayed by weather or discouraged by discomfort. She is very much a man's woman, at home in the wild, even in Scotland or Labrador where the mosquitoes grow like hummingbirds, where there is no shelter but a tent and no lavatory but a bush to be braved as rarely and as quickly as possible. I have seen her telling jokes spirited enough to shock colonels, and singing in a packed public bar, as well as dragging culled stags down from three thousand foot ridges. She is fiercely competitive and no challenge will daunt her if she feels that triumph will be her reward. For example, one particularly remote sea trout loch was rumoured to offer spectacular sport. She made her way there on foot, her equipment carried the nine miles by pony, her only transportation to the bothy by this very remote water. Ridge followed ridge into glorious wilderness, rugged windswept mountainside and the domain of eagles drifting on the thermals above her. The path, centuries old, was worn and shifting and once her pony lost its footing and took a slight fall. But the final ridge was mounted and down into the valley woman and pony went together, a place made safe by inaccessibility and unspoilt for thousands of years.

She unpacked the animal by the side of the loch, very eager to start her fishing. On went the waders and off in a second! Shirley's feet were covered by half scrambled eggs! When the pony had wrong footed, the eggs had cracked, poured down into the water boots and the heat had done the rest.

Virtually all Shirley's paintings are water centred. Even if water is not immediately visible, you sense it flowing deeper down in the valley or just over the watershed. Water texture and colours change constantly and present a huge challenge to the artist. Often Shirley will work on several canvases at once, waiting for lights to reappear, or waiting to recapture particular moments. Constantly she asks our opinion as she fights to portray the essence of an element that is very little given to constriction. This is not a new struggle:

Introduction: Water Passion

''To make anything at all out of all this constant change you have to have five or six canvases on which to work at the same time, and you have to move from one to the other, turning back hastily to the first as soon as the interrupted effect reappears. It's exceedingly hard work, and yet how seductive it is! To catch the fleeting minute or at least its feeling, is difficult enough when the play of light and colour is concentrated on one fixed point, a city scape, a motionless landscape. With water, however, which is such a mobile, constantly changing subject, there is a real problem that is extremely appealing, one that each passing moment makes into something new and unexpected.'' *(Claude Monet)*

We chose the title of this book carefully: to those who know them, rivers are the most joyful places of vivid, spectacular life, or this is how they should be... It is doubtful whether they have been under such awful, joyless threat at any other period in the world's history. On a world scale, we know that the Volga carries enough untreated effluent from the heavy industry of southern Russia to kill all marine life in the Caspian Sea, that the Hudson is floored with mercury and that many of the great eastern rivers are equally, grossly polluted. We fear acid rain and rivers polluted by pesticides and nitrates. We are witnessing a period when sea trout are decimated and when salmon seem to be facing extinction on many rivers. Lowland rivers are abstracted to standing canals and as irrigation lowers water tables, lakes everywhere are becoming depressions of crazed mud. Burbot are a fish species which have completely disappeared from our islands, river roach are vanishing from some systems. Eels around the east coast are found loaded with mercury, shellfish are too poisonous to eat, plaice from the North and Irish seas are infested with sores and cancers.

On the Broads, pleasure cruisers destroy the reed habitat whilst deep drainage leads to the profusion of a lethal algae called Prymnesium.

Introduction: Water Passion

In the highland lochs salmon rearing cages spread disease and forestation and drainage schemes alter critically the traditional burns of spawning trout. In the south, the dredgers work to destroy the natural habitat of fish and water fowl along waterway after waterway.

As every angler realizes his past was richer than his present, these problems are being realized but it is only a notable few who work to address them. On a global scale, the cost of correcting a century of wrongs is stunningly horrendous. Our own problems are considerable as any of the stalwarts from the Atlantic Salmon Trust, the Anglers' Co-operative Association or the Friends of the Earth, for example, will attest to.

We have subtitled the book 'A Celebration'. Perhaps 'A Reminder' would have been more appropriate: we hope it will be a nudge to you to appreciate again these unparalleled places we are privileged to visit and to stir yourselves to fight for them in the future.

A Distant Cast

There are still remote highland rivers that offer salmon fishing of the old sort, before roads were laid and fishing huts became palaces. Here the best pools are approached by trails over the hills made by anglers, deer or stalking ponies. Sometimes the distances are so great that the night is spent in an outlying bothy rather than facing a dozen darkening miles across the moor with a brace of good fish adding weight to the tackle. If the night is still and if it is mild, you pray the hut is sound as the midges will be in and not the most acrid pipe will drive them out. Dinner is the leftovers from the lunch and bed is the bench for the exhausted angler will sleep well enough.

The growing light will wake her though and she will look out over the moorland, dawning with lochans and singing to the sound of the river. Stags are grazing in the dip, lost in the mist, only their bristling antlers showing like an ancient, petrified forest, or a sea of hat racks!

Salmon are showing silver, like angels of the morning and soon a third fish is added to the previous night's brace. In the mild soft morning, though, the midges are becoming so bad that Shirley looks around, strips and swims into the pool to be rid of them. Then she hurriedly dresses and is away, probably back in civilization before the rest of the party have yet breakfasted.

These highland wildernesses must not be taken light-heartedly and there are greater dangers than biting insects. It is easy to be lost in low cloud and disorientated by darkness. One angler returning late stumbled into a bog and was only rescued by the untiring efforts of his labrador to help him pull free. Rain is chilling and never wear tight clothing in it. One lady did so and her jeans shrank so tightly around her that the circulation was cut off and she was stretchered off the hill, never, tragically, to return.

River Shiel, Scotland

The Redds

In December the wind turns to the north and east and the weather finally comes in cold. Heavy sleet falls on to the moors swelling the burns and rising the lochs. From a thousand feet, the hilltops are coated white and the salmon sense a change. Their time of waiting is over and they flood to the burns. Year after year the salmon use the same stream as their ancestors: they spawn in the pools and rapids, on the very redds perhaps, where they were once cast as eggs. It is a period of intensity and the brown water roars in spasms as the thrashing salmon give of their best and their last.

One by one, their duty done, the exhausted fish drop away and their bodies are found by the stalkers leading their ponies up to the hills in the early morning. Dougie, the Head Keeper, bends down and carries a cock fish from the pool where it is struggling, to place it in the open loch. The fish gives a tired slap of its tail, though still strong enough to shower the man's mighty beard in droplets, and is gone. Perhaps that small act of kindness will help the fish back to the sea and on to another cycle of life.

Loch Cluanie, Scotland

View From A Bridge

Can any angler pass a river bridge and not pause to look over to the water beneath? Old bridges are the most complusive, not just because their gentle arches and mellowed stone fits snugly into the landscape but because the currents have been moulded so long by the buttresses that a big, deep downstream pool must, over the years, have been formed. Bridge pools are talked of in hushed whispers. They are magical places. They almost always seem to hold fish.

The very height of the bridge offers a perfect vantage point and you can actually look down vertically onto the fish and, if the sun is well placed, examine every scale and fin beat. If angling is not allowed and the fish remain for long periods undisturbed, it is soon possible to recognise individuals. There is a large, pale chub, the trout with the old, healed up pike scar, the barbel that flashes as it feeds each morning at dawn or the big cock salmon that has lain in the bridge pool for months, waiting for the water to rise.

The village bridge is a magnet. Year round, the young boys lean their bicycles against it and fish into its shade. Young men dive from it through the summer days and at dusk carve the names of their girls into the sandstone. The old boys gather there to smoke, watch the evening rise, and talk ancient gossip before the pub pint and dominoes.

There are famous bridges and hidden ones, large ones and small, old ones and new, but each one is cherished and once seen, spans the angler's imagination from season unto season.

River Dee, Scotland

The Painting Lady of Glencoe

In brooding glen beyond the crag
Awesome peaks watch o'er the hags
Eerie home of hind and stag
Where curlew echoes long and sad.
With paint and brush and artist's pad
The Painting Lady

With rod and line and book of flies
Where salmon run and sea trout lies
'Neath summer's blue or winter skies
On moors where highland clansmen died
In bloody battles ebbs and tides
The Painting Lady

By oceans wild and windy shores
Boats toss around when offshore blows
The spume-clad waves, and few can know
What wrecks and lives they sent below.
She captures them the world to show
The Painting Lady

And set aside the artist's paint
With rifle, scope, a new intent,
With shotgun, dog, a likely stand
Spare cartridge bag, reload to hand,
With Munroe Killer, Willie Gunn,
She'll hold her own, best many a man,
Return once more when sport is done
To tranquil spot with nature one
The Painting Lady

Glencoe, Scotland

19

Yards of Silver

As the big sun sets, the sea trout come in to feed along the shore. The wind is gone and the sea rocks gently with only the murmur of occasional surf. A moon is out and a man treading noisily would see the fish flee like arrows in the phosphorescence. For five hours the sea trout comb the north shore and then the tide begins to flow. In the estuary the water covers the mud flats and the trout follow. Then they find the mouth of the river and the showering shoals of sticklebacks mark their course. As dawn breaks over the big fish, they're forging past the old windmill, through the sleeping village and towards the sweet fresh water of the upper river.

By full daylight, they are lying in the shade of the bridge and the huge willow just downstream. No one thinks to look for them and they are near invisible anyway. Only an occasional magical gleam of silver betrays them as they steady in the current.

Night comes and the fish become more active and feed on the shoals of small fish, the moths and the crawfish that are themselves hunting around the buttresses of the bridge. This was the night that the village boy was out poaching for a brown trout or two. His shadow merged into the greater blackness thrown by the bridge and there he felt safe until his worm was seized and his reel was run down to the spindle in seconds. Something colossal, way beyond his experience, jumped over and over away in the darkness. His rod began to splinter at the ferrule before the line finally gave with a crack that echoed through the night and off the old flint masonry. Mouth dry, his hopes melted like snowflakes in the sea, the boy trudged home fishless.

And it was years before I found the truth of what had smashed me so hopelessly that night.

Cley Mill, Norfolk

21

The Bittern's World

Late afternoon in January, the vast sky is golden from horizon to horizon and the reeds blaze to the sunset. Just a few low clouds carrying snow hang to the north, out over the sea where the spectacular light turns them into glowing castles. Then the stars are out. The light fades and the grasses begin to crackle to the fast falling frost. A pike's tooth moon rises over a perfectly silent world. The night brings cold peace for the bittern, asleep in his feathers, for the bream, eyes blank as the heavens. The darkness freezes on hour after hour marked only by a clock tower on the higher ground and, at last, a slight break in the east.

Up and out at 6am. The marsh white with frost, reeds and sedges sparkling. The boat is frozen in hard. Ice an inch thick coats the dyke though the main flow runs sluggishly open. The sound of breaking ice tinkles over the marshland and the speck of black moves out on the canvas... A boat is rowing briskly up the main river into the broad. It moors. A dark figure stands up against the light. Baits plop out and into the bay by the reeds. The bittern wakes and watches. One reel clicks very slowly. A line coils out over the the mirrored water. The battle is slow and dour and from the way the rod hoops you'd think it was pulling up the bottom itself. Near the boat the big fish tries to tail walk, its mottled back rising to greet the dawn. But the flurry is soon over and the giant is in the net mesh and then on the floor of the boat.

The angler lets out a whoop of joy and fifteen yards away from the reed bed the great brown bittern with the long beak and great trailing legs rises up, soars high into the wind and then beats away on slow flapping wings, low across the shining broad. The pike is unhooked, cradled and held up against the rising sun.

It is a magnificent creature of primitive strength and beauty. Returned, it wallows for a second and then churns off into the shallow water, the bending reeds marking its course.

The Norfolk Broads

The Monster

The tiny trout of a Devon brook possesses magic in every scale and have you ever looked at a fresh, silver, red finned roach, aged around four years old and weighing close to a pound? There is a pearl of nature but, still, it is always the big fish that sets the pulse racing.

Imagine it. A huge bright salmon, its sea feeding done, pushing back to the river of its birth. The journey is a long one but finally the great fish - all four feet long - senses the Spey. It is spring and beat by beat the giant advances towards the distant redds. Now and again it shows like a silver porpoise. Rumours spread. Chances are it feels a hook once, perhaps twice but average Spey tackle and anglers are no match for such a fish in the prime of its life.

The year advances. Through the summer the fish lies in Delagyle beat, glimpsed time to time by the ghillie who know every inch of the river. There is debate amongst them. Some put the fish at fifty pounds and some even higher than that. Whatever, the shadowy presence of such a monster adds tension to every trip and every single cast.

In August it rains, the river rises, the salmon begins to stir in the oxygenated, coloured water. It is evening and a young boy casts out his Devon Minnow. It is taken. Such is the sullen power of the fish that those on the bank are sure the lure is fast on weed, an old cycle or a rock. But now the bottom moves, fast, two hundred yards downstream, past the fishing hut and close to the rapids. The battle has been on for well over half an hour.

A messenger arrives at the lodge, mothers glimpse at their sleeping children, pull on their coats and boots and gather at the water's edge. Torches are flickering on, lighting up the tense, eager faces of the adults and the drained, tired one of the boy. It is dark when the rod gives its final twist and the line flutters free. In saddened silence, the torch beams wander homewards up the hill.

Now it is September and another party arrive fresh on the river. One of the ladies is sleepy still after a long overnight flight and puts up her tackle in a careless way.

River Dee, Scotland

The Monster

Who, after all, catches a fish on the first morning? Her Devon skips out into some deep, fast water, works with the current and suddenly stops. That same ominous power, those same slow uncheckable runs: the tackle groans, the hasty knots slip, then, thankfully, hold.

Once more the salmon heads three hundred yards to the sea, attended by a party, growing as the autumnal sun rises and the mists clear. The angler is Lilla Rowcliffe and her cousin, Jim Deterding, takes the net. He senses that the big fish cannot hold the bottom as it did, the current can now push it off balance, that the end is near. He takes up his position as a great shape emerges towards him, to the light. He gasps. The fish dwarfs his net. For what seems an age, he wrestles to secure the salmon in the mesh. He feels panic growing above him then he lifts and turns round to meet a stunned silence. It takes two to carry the fish to the hut where it is weighed at 45lbs. 3oz.

The epic is over: a mammoth fish is dead and defeated in nature's purpose. Now it is a trophy for the family wall, generation unto generation. The day progresses with perhaps some envy here and there but a good deal of genuine congratulation, for Lilla Rowcliffe that day caught a historic fish. She saw a creature few of us are ever privileged to get at. I have known males, fanatical men admittedly, whose lives have been changed by the capture of a leviathan, but I suspect Lilla thinks of that great day - 10.30am. the 22nd September - just now and again and smiles. There will be a glow all her lifetime, deep down in her heart.

The dividing line between this or any other monster being landed or going free could not be thinner. When I was ten a huge brown trout sipped in my dry fly at dusk and took me up and down its remote Pennine reservoir. Somehow I kept in control enough to tire it, though I was white knuckled and shaking. But the fish was too large for the net and as it wallowed there the fly sprang from its top lip and it returned wearily to the depths. I felt no greater disaster could befall me.

River Tay, Scotland

The Monster

As a grown man, I lost a giant mahseer in the river Ganges after a titanic struggle that had led me half a mile across stones and rapids. Physically I was exhausted but emotionally I was shattered. The moon was rising, it was my last day on the river and all the old despair overwhelmed me.

It was my Indian guide who made sense of the loss. It is no disgrace to be beaten by the forces of nature. To be humbled by a mighty fish is infinitely preferable to a savaging by hurricane, flood or leopard! Rather rejoice that 'Mother Ganga' still holds such monsters and having battled with one and lost, return is obligatory!

He was quite right. A year later I had saved, planned and was back under the Indian sun, nursing at last my own monster mahseer.

River Spey, Scotland

Forgotten River

The river runs in a mountain wilderness, from the last century, reached only by an ancient stalking path. There are no roads and mercifully, no forestry, nothing but the glen stretching ahead in the misty morning. The day is damp and clammy and walking is hard work through the swirls of mist sweeping down from the hillside, freckling the small river with moisture. For a mile past, the water could be crossed in a single jump, everywhere it is fordable and all the forecasts had been gloomy before I left. All the bar room anglers had said it was too small, too slow, too acidic and that they themselves had never even bothered to make such a wasted trek. My own hopes are low.

I stop finally at a very high pool towards the head of the glen. There are deer watching from the skyline, the only souls seen in four hours of wandering. This is it. I draw breath and cast. A small Peter Ross is taken within seconds. The fish is eight inches long and creamy fat. The pool delivers six fish and the second eight. And so it goes through the afternoon until the first traces of evening warn me to follow the river back to the distant track and civilization. Seventy-three fish in all have been banked, generally between four and six ounces but one was a monster of nearly two pounds. Seventy-one had gone back and there are just two in my pocket.

I lay them out on the bar. ''Yes, that's all. A twenty- five mile walk for those two.''

I lie: we all know what men can do to Eden.

River Dionard, Scotland

The Last Burbot

On a floodplain in the eastern counties stands a very old, very gnarled willow tree. It leans precariously into the winds for every winter of its life, cattle have gathered in its lee to escape the horizontal, wet westerlies. They have pushed it and butted it and gnawed at it but it stands still beside the dyke that runs into the flatland river. Nor is the dyke itself in a great deal better shape than the tree, half choked with reeds and rubbish. It is rare to see anyone on the banks now, though a small pool remains in front of the willow where experienced anglers still go on occasion to catch a bream or two.

Henry is one of them and though he is not beyond late middle age, he remembers that pool as a very different place. As a younger man he used to catch bream, rudd and pike a plenty up and down the dyke and at dusk he would settle under the willow with a hook full of worms. The town clock would chime ten and fron then on till midnight he could expect an eel pout or two. That is what he called them Burbot, in fact, they were. These were the perculiar, eel shaped fish with a cod like head that once was so sought after through the eastern counties. Now they have gone. Henry has not seen one since the 1960's and he was about the last ever to catch one. He placed it back into that pool beneath the willow where it vanished like the entire species. No one knows why and apart from Henry and a few friends, no one cares that a once common species should find modern conditions intolerable. Soon, though, the willow will collapse and choke the pool and the last testament to the burbot will be gone for ever.

A Broadland Willow

Impossible Rivers

These are invisible rivers that have no more colour, taste or smell than the air itself. The chalk stream is so pure, so radiant, so afire with icelight that every trout fin, fleck and scale is washed and polished until it shines. The weed furls like a lace curtain on the breeze, the pondskater hangs like a spider on its web and trout hover magically in airy nothingness like humming-birds. The chalk stream does not screen or separate a man from his trout and often it is only apparent as an element at all because the current crinkles it, a coot splashes it in defiance or best of all, because a trout dimples it with a kissing rise.

You watch the one and a half pound brown trout that has occupied the lie behind a tress of ranunculus since the late spring and you realize that there are a thousand and one reasons that neither you, nor anyone, will catch him. That fish knows the exact muscle of the current and how it lifts up a nymph or escorts the hatch fly on its surface. The artificial must not only look exact but it must behave exact and that is almost impossible to accomplish. Your presentation must be excellent to make him even drift from his position a few inches and it takes near perfection to draw him to the taking point... and even then, on the brink, he will pause for that last fateful look and remain free.

Dusk possibly offers the only chance. A mild close evening with cloud cover will keep down the light and the fly hatch will be intense enough to dull his caution. The frenzy to feed and feed grows in him. There is competition from other fish and this breeds real haste. Suddenly, to him, your fly looks good enough. Up he comes, steady on his pectorals, gauging the distance. He flicks his tail. His mouth is opening. You blink your eye, there is a splash of water and nothing. The artificial floats on and your trout will be that much harder, if possible, in the future.

River Kennett, Hungerford

Colours of Spring

Norrie, the giant builder from Glasgow, emerged from a snowstorm that engulfed the river and flung himself down in a hollow to escape the rising wind. Even those hands used to sites all over the lowlands were red raw with the cold. He took a few swigs from his hipflask and prepared to settle in for as long as the storm should last. But it was spring and the squall went as quickly as it had come and soon the sun burst in, igniting the gorse above his head to yellow fire. Norrie picked himself up, walked over the carpet of soft melting snow and prepared to cast. The sun glinted off the big silver spoon and burst the water into flames where it splashed. The river was dazzling under the brilliant blue sky, reflecting the crisp white of the hills. The big man steadily worked pool after pool, his boots avoiding the carpets of spring flowers, his body brushing through the budding birches, bark bright silver in the sunlight. In the stream, the stones were polished by the snow water, liquid blues and browns, speckled like underwater eggs. He paused by an emerald waterfall and cast into the plumes of glittering bubbles. A small butter bellied trout bumped the spinner with his head and told it to clear off. This was his pool.

Norrie reeled in and climbed the hillside to the hotel. He came out by the churchyard spangled with daffodils. The bar was awash with sunlight. No one had caught a salmon but a couple had been seen, silver cutlasses cutting through the white water.

"You won't be going out again, Norrie?" The landlord pointed to the head of the glen where more black snow clouds rolled. Already a veil of white was drawing down to the hotel. Such is the startling springtime of the highlands.

River Dee, Scotland

The Wormer

There are the open, spate rivers of the grouse moors gushing through the heather where there is always a wind blowing. They may be poor in food but they are rich in trouting interest. The walk is often long and lonely to tiny pools that are peaty, overhung and dark or to bright stickles some six inches deep. The trout are small, and electric spotted. They can be fished for with the fly and will snatch at teams of small flashers or dimple at dusk to a size twenty Black Gnat.

It is just as difficult though on the clear brooks to fish the upstream worm, a method that teaches like no other really can. The worm fisher must place the bait with absolute precision to the fish in its lie and must know intimately where and how the trout live. The worm fisher is like a cartographer, mapping every stone, every current and every water ledge. He reads the river more happily than his palm. He is the stalker, the osprey eyed master of concealment. He moves heron slow and everything about his fishing is controlled. His cast is pin point perfection. He keeps constant contact with his worm for he knows any slack could lead to a gorged bait and a dead fish. He mends the line to every whim of the current, or the breeze on the surface and every vibration is transmitted down the rod to his fingers, senses and brain. No angler knows the spirit of the upland river better than the worm fisher. And no method better deserves a small, fine, fighting trout.

Bowes Moor, Yorkshire

Bothy Life

On the far northern estate of a wealthy Dutchman great interest and attention is bestowed upon the land, the water and the creatures that live in them. I happened to be there with a friend one October as the deer rut took place, waiting for the salmon to run to the redds in the loch. Our purpose was to catch salmon by rod or net, to tag them, radio track them and follow their every movement at this vital stage of their life cycle. All our information would be gathered and sent to scientists who would then interpret our work as best they could.

Accomodation was a bothy, so old and so nearly derelict that it shook with every blow of wind... and this was a terrible period of storms. Day after day we dragged ourselves across the moor, over the loch, up and down the river in cold, stinging rain, knowing that all there was to come were nights of dampness under a tossing, sleepless, corrugated iron roof.

Then there were periods of beauty. One day the sun rose through a flawless blue sky and the loch mirrored the mountains in perfect detail. We saw their peaks dusted in snow and the stags themselves that previously had roared unseen at the clouds. Our boat shone white on the water, flies hatched and trout eagerly took their last meal before the winter. In mid-loch occasional salmon arked silver in the sunlight. It was a dazzling day before the cloud once more marched in from the west. The wind rose and by mid afternoon gusts were whipping the water into hundred foot spumes. Indeed, what was spindrift and what was rain was impossible to tell on this numbing, terrifying journey home,

It was midnight and yet another storm gradually ceased and from my bed I could see stars in the velvet. Outside frost was falling after the rain and beads of ice shone in a strange, vibrating light. Above, the Northern Lights stretched horizon to horizon. It was like a carnival, like some bizarre light show of the gods; all sliding, pulsating patterns and throbbing colours that reflected off the glassy loch. The stags continued to roar and

River Moriston, Scotland

a wisp of smoke from the dying stove left the chimney before it sadly bowed to the east. One by one the stars switched off and the lights were cloaked in cloud. The frost had gone before the first raindrops fell once more and the west wind began to howl.

It was December when the salmon finally began to run the burns and work began sexing fish, taking scales and measurements and marking down the redds. But now the moors were awash with water, the whole world was grey and deserted apart from the gallant, coloured salmon making their final journey.

The River Gruniard

The Buddha

The glory of rural England is locked in its great landed estates and the wonderful halls with fine porches, mellowed red brick facades, turreted gables, mullioned windows and lilied moats; in the estate villages, with the bell towers, the stableyards, the keepers' cottages, the lodges covered in honeysuckle and the walled gardens of old asparagus beds and stately vines; in the beehives buried in the orchards, in the dovecotes, the summer houses, the chestnut mares and the Jersey cows plagued by the flies from the long hay; in the clipped hedgerows of yew and privet, in pleached fruit trees and limes and in the ancient oaks of the great deer parks. Though the world has changed around them, though the life of the twentieth century has hammered at their walls and gates, many still survive, independent and held by the old family line.

They all have lakes, sheets of water designed and built for beauty in the future - moon shaped pools, willowed islands that weep in the breeze, old boathouses, thatched reflections in the water, old dam walls and forests of reed that fire in the setting sun. They hold tench and rudd and some have carp that grow as large as young boys and wallow in the silt and weed for over half a century of their lives. In the Gardener's Lake lives an enormous carp. Nowadays, it is not unusual for big carp around the country to be so well known that they have names. 'She', 'Raspberry', 'Heather' and 'Eric' are all names of fish from the modern age that have been pursued for most of their adult lives by eager anglers. Sometimes the quest becomes a war of attrition between a fish and an angler who has sworn to be successful. The battle can last for seasons and the fish can still emerge successful and uncaught. It is a little the same in this lake.

I have called my carp the Buddha, because he is serene, a smooth golden brown and infinitely above my capacity for comprehension. The Gardener's Lake is in itself a temple for him, with willows for walls and lilies and pink crowfoot serving as mosaics. It lies in the top fold of the valley and has fine views over the downs to the red-bricked village and beyond to the sea. The lake has housed the Buddha for decades but no one knows how he came to be there. He is the most secretive of fish. I am not convinced the Buddha has ever been caught or indeed ever will.

For one whole summer, I watched the Buddha and he never moved from a table-top sized hole in the weed. I realised that for over three months he ate nothing but microscopic waterfleas which he hoovered into his great pink mouth hour upon hour. In fact, a bait larger than a pinhead seemed to repulse him and I ended the year quite baffled by him.

Kelling Lake, Norfolk

The Buddha

Never mind. The year was not wasted. Every time the Buddha approached a bait of mine I felt an overwhelming surge of adrenalin. My blood pulsed in my temples, my mouth went dry and inevitably, my heart would sink as he turned away again into the weeds. ''Tomorrow'', I always told myself, ''There is tomorrow.''

In truth though, if the Buddha were ever to lie in my net, tomorrow might as well never come. The moment my hands run along the Buddha's flank of gold will be a full stop in my angling life. No. I am content to follow him for seasons yet and providing I never catch him my dream will always remain.

Kelling Lake, Norfolk

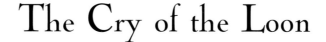

The Cry of the Loon

A flight of starlings rises, dips, turns broadside and flattens out again in a vast aerial manoeuvre. The thousand starlings, in perfect time to a tune only they know, dance the last of the daylight away. In a sweeping curtain, they drape the lake and again as one, settle into the gold drenched marshes to the east.

It is a magnificent sunset: blues, crimsons, oranges and yellows all in a cauldron of fire. The margins of the river begin to fill in with shadows and then it is night. Above, the heron crawks, his ragged shape caught in descent against the moon. His entry at the tail of the pool does not dislodge a stone or send even a ripple over the water. He comes like death in the night.

Dawn again: the iceberg swans with cygnets of snowcloud down drift through the mist. The grebe, pure dagger of white, the kingfisher, the dippers, the divers, the robin by the boot of the winter time piker; the swallows and the swifts that skim the pools; the wagtail skipping the rapids and the cold eyed cormorant; the high trails of geese, the battling coots, the woodpigeons that sing all day long and the owl that calls at dusk: the loon that cries over the silent water, the soul of the dawn.

And only the angler sees them all.

The Loon (Great Northern Diver)

For the Love of Salmon

For many decades, many men have devoted their energies to the preservation of salmon. Whilst other species have suffered from a declining environment during the same period, it is the salmon that has been fought for most furiously. Why? It cannot simply be for monetary reasons. Though no one doubts the financial importance of this amazing fish to the Scottish economy in particular, there must be more to our deep urge to keep the salmon stocks viable. Our need for salmon must be for more than food either. Farm salmon are here forever and though perhaps not as delicately flavoured or as nutritious as the wild fish, they are an acceptable substitute. Again, though no one doubts that to catch a silver Atlantic salmon is one of the pinnacles in field sport, the screeching reel and the hooped rod alone do not explain the passion of the preservationists. The need is very much deeper than the thrill alone.

Perhaps we fear shame...Shame that if our world can no longer support this most glorious of fish, we have quite obviously failed as a race. Each time a salmon leaps a fall it is visible proof that our world can, perhaps, still be saved. To the angler or to any lover of nature, the wild salmon is a talisman. If we lose it, we lose the whole spirit of the wild and angling would become a tame put-and-take kind of sport indeed.

In practical terms, no one has done more for the preservation of salmon than Lord Thurso. Shirley Deterding's recollections of him and his work remain vivid.

"Into the hotel strode the Laird of Thurso - a true highland chieftain in all senses of the word. His size and his presence filled every inch of space and his big welcoming smile and firm, warm handshake made me feel instantly at ease. His son accompanied him and with these two magnificent kilted men I walked into the bar of the Ulbster Arms Hotel to sit and discuss the Thurso river. I was lucky enough to have an invitiation from Lord Thurso to fish for salmon on his private beat the following day and I was naturally anxious to learn all I could about this famous northern river operating so successfully under the one management and ownership.

The river is controlled and run by the family estate and sees a balance between profitable estuary netting and rod fishing on the river. The water is divided into thirteen beats, twelve of which the rods fish in rotation thus taking two consecutive weeks to fish the pools in their entirety. Obviously I have heard alot of controversy about the merits and

River Tay, Scotland

disadvantages of netting and most fishermen take the view that less fish in the river mean less fish to catch. The management argument is that more income from the netting means more money to spend on the upkeep and maintenance of the river. In today's climate where the necessity of making an estate pay means taking maximum advantage of the natural amenities, a good balance is most important. This, I think, has been ideally achieved on the Thurso because of single ownership, where the degree of netting, fishing, and re-stocking have been carefully balanced to get the best of all worlds. Lord Thurso also justified his reasoning by telling me the sad tale of one year when the nets were left off and all the salmon run went up the river. The pools became so overfull with fish that when the river dropped they died in their hundreds from overcrowding and lack of  oxygen and had to be scooped out daily and buried. Perhaps this was a fluke of nature but on these small northern rivers which rely heavily on spate rises to keep up their flow, there could be some justification in controlling the number of running fish as long as a generous re-stocking programme is maintained.''

Indeed, Lord Thurso's own paper in that important document 'The Status of the Atlantic Salmon in Scotland', compiled by The Institute of Terrestrial Ecology, makes plain the importance of balance. ''Let us begin by asking ourselves what constitutes management when the term is applied to a salmon fishery resource. In general, it must comprise all actions designed to ensure the maximum production, exploitation, continuance and improvement of the resource and the co-ordination of these sometimes conflicting aims.'' Lord Thurso went on to make several central points. Waters need to be free from undue competition and therefore he electrofishes brown trout from the spawning streams and removes them to nearby lochs. Estuary netting he does not mind providing enough fish get through and up the river and for this reason he imposes weekly and daily closed times to make the whole process what he calls ''mildly inefficient''. What he would ban is drift netting. This is far too efficient and destroys the delicate balance that is so essential. The salmon that do return to the Thurso find an ever improving river there to greet

River Dee, Scotland

them. Fifty percent of the pools are man made and a dam has been constructed on Loch More which will prolong the effects of spates and river rises. In the upper waters the number of redds are increased and made accessible to breeding fish. Those inaccessible are stocked artificially with fry taken from his own local lochs. Like any successful business, management on the Thurso depends on eternal vigilance, on the stocks, on poaching, on anglers and on netting stations. In this way Lord Thurso has made his river an example to the world.

River Dee, Scotland

The Back Cast

"Fishing is a real test of character. Your spirits are either on top of a mountain or in the depth of a pit. There are many sufferings... The fly in the small of your back. A disintegrated lunch, bulls, wasps' nests, moorhens at the wrong moment, cockchafers in your eye, the cast which doubles back, the matches which you have left at home and worst of all, water in your wader ."

Plunkett Greene was not the first angler to realize there has to be more to fishing than fish. He might have mentioned sleet on the back of the neck, the nettles in the summer, the fly cast around the alder branch and the day that you sink slowly and inescapably into an Irish bog.

When success is as far off as the moon you, I, even Shirley will become careless... Her back cast hooked a young bullock under the tail, sharp in his most vulnerable parts. The goggle-eyed beast's first run took the reel to the drum and it was an hour later and two beats downstream that Shirley, the farmer, the ghillie, a labourer, two anglers, a small boy on a bicycle and three gun dogs 'tailed' the creature and retrieved a very 'Hairy Mary'.

River Deveron, Scotland

Out of Constable

There is no more gentle a sight in angling than a roach river of the old sort. The dredger has hacked the guts out of most of them, though, and they are now more in memory than reality, caught in the soft focus of a sepia photograph or the tranquility of a Constable painting. There are places, though, where the ghosts linger and the present is not too much at odds with the past... Bintree Mill dominates the scene, afloat like a great white galleon on a hazy floodplane. Though its working life has stopped, the building still stands proud, throwing its shadow over the sluices and the deep, mysterious pools beneath. Down river of the building, the river leaves these pools in streams that dance with dace and sunlight. The water is shallow, quick and veiled with white willows. There are good trout still, wild browns that breed at the tail of the weir in the autumn. Kingfishers hunt their fry and the herons can find their fill of gudgeon or small eels in the springtime.

But it is the river upstream, ponded, deep and slow, where the roach have for generations thrived. Though the dredger has visited there over the years, it has not straightened the river to a ruler and it is on the deep, oily bends that shoals of big roach still remain. Summer and winter alike you fish for them at dawn or at dusk with large lumps of breadflake on the river bed. Sometimes fish roll in front of you in heavy boils of red and silver and you know that bites are not far away.

A fourteen inch roach is a lovely sight held under the moon or the rising sun. It is a fish of the marsh, of the barn owl, of graceful, draping trees and of peace and tranquillity. But let us remember, such places and sights are not common today and pray to God that Bintree is never lost.

Bintree Mill, Norfolk

Michael's River

Over the waters of Michael's River a canoe emerges from the dawn's mist. As it closes, you see a magical painted salmon on its prow. Droplets of water run tearfully down it, revitalizing its colours, as though the real fish is caught a second above the water line in mid leap.

The winter was over, a terrible period in Labrador when temperatures can drop to minus forty degrees centigrade and when the fishing lodge is lost under the snows right to its chimney pots, and now the thaw was slow. The bay was a tangle of icebergs, ghostly blue against the bright skies and fishing had been slow. It was before dawn when Shirley left the warmth of the building to face the cool winds blowing off the ice but there was an incoming tide which could just bring success. She walked the sand, fresh marked by bear, wolf and caribou and watched whales feeding in the bay as the sun rose. The light rod and small single hooked fly looked puny against the might of the bay but she kept working them along the shore. Suddenly there were fish there before her. The fly was snatched and a big salmon ran for his saviour, the sea. The sun was well up when it finally slid on to the sand and so beautiful did it look there that she sat down, exchanged rod for brush and made a little masterpiece on the only canvas available to her.

Michael's River, Labrador

Ferox!

Scottish lochs hold more mysteries than monsters alone in their depths. Deep down, hundreds of feet into the void, hang the vast shoals of Arctic char, moving on the currents, grazing on microscopic foods. Half a century ago, Patrick Chalmers traced the char back to "The push of the ice packs and the glacier waters of the Age of Ice. And when the pale blue glacial rivers, in the terrible days of the ice melt, could run no further, some of their waters remained to mingle here and again with lakes, tarns and lochans, in the deep beds that their mother Ice made for them in her final labour. And therein stayed the char, men say, and there he stays still."

Few men have seen a char and not one of those who has will ever forget their brilliant colours: the blues, the greens, the pinks and the purples, borrowed, as Chalmer says, from the Northern Lights themselves.

A study of the char leads to the discovery of an even more magnificent creature. The ferox is a strain of brown trout that has developed great size and power by feeding almost exclusively off the char shoals.

Fewer men still have ever seen a ferox and most believe the legends that paint them as black, big headed, lanky-bodied degenerates. This is one of angling's saddest delusions. A highland loch. Sunset. A ferox lies on the boards of the boat. Keep your eyes off it if you can. A neat head, a muscle packed body with paddle sized fins. And all over, a cascade of jet black spots that paint the fish as one of nature's finest creations.

And even sadder is the slander that ferox fight like sacks of manure. Stamina is built up by their constant wandering in search of the char and speed by their dashes into the fleeing shoal. Hook one and he will come close to the boat like a puzzled lamb. He will even rise to within twenty feet of the surface until he sees your gawping reflection. Then he will dive, seemingly forever. On and on the battle goes, your hands are numb and your shoulders ache. Probably he will come up through the water as quickly as he went down and start to leap. That is when your heart stops, when you have the greatest brown trout in the country airborne in front of you. Then you know the ferox has the heart and the nobility of a savage.

Loch Cluanie, Scotland

Ferox!

It is hardly surprising that the Victorians found such excitment in the ferox and pioneered techniques for them. Many old records suggest that there were far more of them a century ago. In decent conditions, anything between 4 and 8 fish a week could be considered normal - as many as ferox specialists today can hope to see in ten years! Average sizes appeared to be larger too, with several over 17lbs reported most decades. The Victorians even claimed a massive 39½ pounder as their record.

The reasons for this decline can only be guessed at. It does seem certain that numbers of small trout have fallen throughout the Highlands. Where once catches were measured in bucketfuls now cups would do! Shortages of prey fish are bound to affect ferox populations.

Nor can increased angling pressure help. Few ferox are returned: as it takes twelve or more years for a ferox to top ten pounds a fish removed is not quickly replaced.

River Cluanie, Scotland

Estate Lakes

Ninety percent of water in the world is salt water. Of fresh water, two percent is frozen in the ice caps and a further .59% is buried in the aquifer. Only .007% of the world's fresh water is contained in lakes and the vast majority of even this tiny percentage is concentrated in the vast sheets of Superior, Michegan, Victoria, of Baikal. Lowland lakes are not even teardrops beside the likes of Ness, of Constance, or of Mask.

Yet, these tiny waters, so often cradled in landed estates, are special places. Here, nature and man have collaborated together, waterscaping valleys with magic. A great hall without water is one without life: at Versailles, an army was deployed to alter the course of a river over fifty miles so that it would water the garden there. Thousands of men died but the attempt had to be made for without this essential element, the park could never be complete, like an eye that does not see or a sky eternally clouded. Fountains, cascades, pools and streams are the very breath of life to formal gardens, but even more vital is the distant glimpse of the lake, winking in the sunshine of an arcadian afternoon.

Two hundred, even one hundred years ago, labour was cheap: shovel and sweat redirected streams, built dams, boathouses and islands and planted sweeps of white willows. Great trouble was taken in stocking the waters with rare species of fish like carp or catfish brought from the Continent or even bass from America. Father to son, the lakes were handed down, enjoyed, maintained and even improved. Today, perspiration costs pounds per bead and these beautiful droplets are gradually silting back into the marshes from whence they came. Springs are weakening, reeds are encroaching and year by year more and more of these little stars of water are going out never to twinkle again.

A Norfolk Stillwater

An Angler Remembers

It was high summer and we set out early in the morning for a long walk along the sea arm westwards. A bright sun had risen over the hills behind us, flooding the saltwater to the right with blue light and picking the path out bright, whether over moor or through low lying marsh. Occasional groups of Scots pine dotted the way and a marten scurried, lean and long, across the path. Seals played in the water, buzzards drifted in the sky and the ever warming air was full of droves of insects.

We walked about six miles, tackle and provisions becoming ever heavier, and then we reached the bay. The large house there was locked and shuttered but the bothy in the garden, mercifully, was open to all. We left the gear and ran, I remember, over the meadows to the seatrout river that flowed in from the bay and wound a mile or two towards the mountains that crowded round the skyline. We had been told the river was clear, fast and deep: it sparkled and it screamed 'seatrout' to us and chattered,

"Come at sunset and I'll prove it!"

We ate a large, late lunch and dozed in the bothy through the long afternoon. Flies droned amongst the food scraps left by walkers and a mouse kept busy under the sink. We stirred as the sun lay on the horizon and the tide began to advance up the shore to push against the current of our river. We had some soup and a dram as we waited and watched. Occasional splashes in the bay, closing on the mouth of the river, gave us the greatest hope. Then the gold went off the water, at dusk a vivid violet set in and we walked off to the pools.

The night was very short. Dawn began to creep in around three and an hour later all sport was over. We returned to the bothy to sleep but

River Gruniard, Scotland

all I could do was doze, unable to clear from my mind the image of the five pounder, glittering under the moon, running with the fast water, unconquerable, it seemed, half the night long. I got up from the bed and looked at it lying on the shelf above the sink, still silver, gleaming in the growing light. Half an hour passed and still I marvelled at its shape and colour, occasionally running my fingertip over the flawless flanks and fins.

We ate him later that day with cold potatoes and toasted him with white wine. But those were the old days when our rivers were privileged to receive the huge runs of silver trout, before another of nature's creatures began to relent at last to the pressures of this impossible world.

River Gruniard, Scotland

The Magic of the Findhorn

Twilight was darkening the river and soothing the sound of the water, even muffling the splash of the salmon in the pool before us. I was trembling as I held the rod, all my attention focused on the line as though it was some magical umbilical cord to the pulsating life below. I could not remember when last I had been so engrossed in my sport, so utterly oblivious to anything in the world outside it.

It was a shock when my ghillie, my friend, whispered, ''Hush'', for I had not said a word and had even forgotten his existence. He beckoned me up the path from the pool and I followed him through the shadows, up to the meadows where the trees drew apart and let in more of the last light.

Sandy pulled me down into the bracken and pointed out over the grasses that were already thickening with mist. Twenty yards from us a young dog fox and two heifers were prancing and dancing. The fox barked, snarled, leapt into the air and rolled on his back. The heifers snorted, hooved the ground and made tentative head butting charges before backing off to avoid a blaze of claws and snap of teeth. For some minutes the game continued until, suddenly scenting us, the fox melted and was gone into the gloom. We could only guess; the young fox was after the first of the night's rabbits and alarmed the heifers who jumped into the attack; or, perhaps they had picked up his scent as he crossed the field, the river on his mind as a place to drink and find a water vole or two.

Sandy agreed it was too late for salmon but reassured me that dawn was not far off. He stripped the fly off my line and put on a hook and a great wriggling worm and cast it into the deep slow water below the rock face.

''Eels,'' he said. The moon rose and danced on the black water of the pool ringed by rising parr, making the gravel glitter. In the magic of the Findhorn night, it was easy to muse on Hina, the moon maiden, who bathed in such a pool each day and was caressed by an eel as she did

River Findhorn, Scotland

so. At length, the eel threw its skin and became a beautiful youth and her lover.

Sandy laughed. ''And my father wore the skin of an eel around his upper legs to keep away the cramps in cold weather and his father used to put a live eel in his pints of beer to keep away the drunkenness!'' The eels we actually caught that night Sandy fried in the hut and were eaten not much before the early summer sun rose over the Findhorn again and we could begin to fish in earnest once more.

River Findhorn, Scotland

The Frozen Marsh

That winter the winds came constantly from the north and with nothing but sea between the coast and the Artic, they felt bitterly cold and carried constant sleet and snow. The creeks froze over each low tide and on the flow, sheets of broken ice drifted against the boats, the quayside and into the dykes of the salt marshes. The corpse of a whale, a dark brown leviathan of a thing, was washed up on to the beach, kingfishers were found starved and many of the coastal birds were driven to forage in the harvested carrot fields. When the reed cutters had their food breaks, the normally shy tits and warblers came to them, fighting over scraps of bread and cheese.

Strangely, the only people to profit were the cod fishermen. For weeks, shoals of big fish fed along the shingle bank and on a night tide especially, anything up to a dozen of the creamy cod could be landed. They fought furiously amongst the ice cold breakers and great was the action amidst the hissing Tilly lamps. Digging the lugworms for bait was the hardest thing for the sand was frozen with the wind and the worms had gone very deep. Each digger could be seen for miles on the mud flats, surrounded by a haze of white as the gulls and terns jostled for scraps of broken lug. Then another squall brought snow in off the sea and the whole marsh was lost in a whirl of white.

Thornham Creek, Norfolk

The Explorer

Angling has always had its explorers, men and women whose lust for big fish has led them to sometimes exotic, frequently dangerous places. Such a man, a friend, travelled India and Nepal for a year, using native transport, lodgings and food. He fell sick and became haunted by fears of failure but in the end he found mahseer - the great Asiatic carp - and opened up rivers all but forgotten since Independence.

He searched Africa for giant tigerfish, broke his ribs and nearly lost a companion to malaria. The same spirit took him to Iceland, not to the highly priced salmon rivers, but to the lonely interior. He trekked several river systems, fishing as he went and living off the trout that he caught. Sport was as spectacular as the deserted landscape itself and from the numbers and size of the trout he saw, he guessed he must have been the first for years to cast a fly into most of the pools. What impressed him most though, was that this is the purest form of fishing, when a man, like an osprey or an otter, takes just enough from nature to survive. Then the angler is not a sportsman but a hunter again, reliving how it all began.

Langa River, Iceland

Blind As An Eagle

He was born in the glen and began exploring it as soon as he could walk. As a child he had a pet foxcub, used to feed wild martens and be able to walk right up to deer in the winter. He had no time or interest in school for he wanted only to be on the hills and he left as soon as he could to become a ghillie on the river. His knowledge was invaluable. He knew every salmon lie, every hill lochan, every twist in the burns and every depth change in the lochs. He was a beautiful caster, a crack shot and a sinuous oarsman. He became famous for, if fish were there, then his gentlemen would be catching them. However, he often had scant respect for those who employed him. He could be difficult and he always took the credit for any capture. It was well known that you couldn't trust him with a bottle or a girl but his unparalleled knowledge and love of the glen saw him through scrape after scrape.

When the war came his skills with the gun were required. He was captured and set to work in an eastern mine. There he feigned blindness and though the Germans put him through every test, often painful, he never flinched. Finally, they shipped him to England and he landed in the south, still 'blind'. He was taken back to the glen and he was given a pension for life. As soon as the back of authority was turned, blind as an eagle, he continued his work as before. To the day he died he could see a dram on a mountain top five miles away and not a living creature in the glen ever escaped that hawk-like gaze.

River Dionard, Scotland

The Leaper

The first snows were on the hills and the temperature had fallen dramatically. The salmon were now running in numbers and some were caught in traps set by the Fisheries Department so that the fish could be stripped and their eggs artificially reared. Salmon of all sizes were caught and carried from the river in wheelbarrows to be placed in tanks that were fed by a torrent of water from a six inch diameter pipe.

For a while the salmon would lie on their sides exhausted, their gills working rapidly. Then they would right themselves and sulk for a short while on the bottom of the tank but, as soon as they were refreshed, they would rise up and begin to leap at the solid plume of water that fell from the tap. The force was massive, so great that I could hardly hold my own palm against it, but this did not deter the fish from soaring again and again in their futile passion.

I spent much of the afternoon watching these fish and looking at their blank, expressionless eyes, that were always fixed on the flowing water.

Theirs was an implacable determination. This was an unquestioning, unquenchable, unstoppable drive to follow water to its beginnings.

This is an urgency no human can feel; unqualified, totally focused, without diversions of any sort. Let us be humble when, with our nets and our lines, we try to stop them.

As dusk fell I walked away but I could hear the splashes of the salmon in the gloom behind me, loud over the roar of the river and the bellow of the stags rutting on the hillside.

A Tributary of the River Dee, Scotland

Celtic Pike

From a distant loch word came of some incredible pike, huge fish of over four feet long that when hungry, would take pork chops and even slabs of dead sheep! There is something about pike that inspires gross exaggeration but there seemed just enough truth in this tale to justify a journey. After all, if half the story were true then there would be memorable piking.

The week began with sharp frosts, bright sunlight and flurries of snow that coated the hills. Though this was typical beautiful autumn weather in the Highlands, it could hardly have been worse for a pike man and I began to despair. Fishless still after four days I began to wonder if I should have changed bait to a haunch of ham! Suddenly, though, things changed. A mild westerly with low, damp cloud and a grey mildness turned the loch into a pewter puddle. Immediately pike began to take deep fished copper spoons. They were not as large as the fish I had hoped for but they were lean and fit and leapt like dervishes.

A little after dawn the next day however something quite different hit the hooks. For a minute I was quite sure I was snagged and I actually reversed the boat over the fish itself before it moved away slowly and steadily up the loch.

From then onwards, the fish took me pretty well where it wanted, towing the boat slowly against the rippled water. For fifteen minutes I never saw the fish, never raised it from the bottom and when finally it shook itself free, all I had as proof were two bent and busted trebles and a deeply tooth-gouged plug. I sat and shook for a long time in the well of the dinghy, dreading to think of the size of the pike I had lost. I still fear that it was one of those highland monsters that is landed every half century or so, a fish that would have made my name safe in the record books for posterity.

The Isle of Mull, Scotland

Questions of Silver

A child looks over a bridge in the grey light of morning and a shoal of grilse graces the pool. There are twenty fish, perhaps more, hanging in the deep dark corners, under outcrops of rock or hidden by reflections in the forest. From above, every fish is identical: there is not an inch, a fin or a scale to separate them. Every one must be within an ounce or two of five pounds and each is as silver as the moon. Only one stands apart; a fish attacked by a seal or an otter with the wound unhealed, a gape of red flesh showing clearly.

The child turns to his father. Have these fish been together since their eggs were dropped on the same redds? Were they parr playing together in the thin bright water and then smolts, swimming out to sea as one great shoal? Did they travel together, losing companions to bass, cod seals and seabirds as they went? Did they feed as a shoal on the rich harvest of the sea and, as one, feel the urge to return to the freshwater of their collective birth? Will they spawn together, brother and sister on the redds of their beginning and rot back as one corpse to their parent river?

Under cover of the next night's darkness, the salmon left the pool, a shoal of question marks working up river towards the final solution.

The River Naver, Scotland

In stages, the fish travelled the summer river marooned in pools, waiting for rain to ease their way forward again. One fish fell to a bright orange fly, another in a poacher's snare and two to dangled worms during a sudden flood. The salmon lost their freshness along with their companions and the year began to fade.

Out walking in the new year, the child came across what had been four of the grilse rotting together on a shingle bank. He hesitated before the reek of death but his curiosity overwhelmed him and he reached out to lift one. It crumbled in his hands and fell apart onto the sand.

The boy stood up. Why is there such waste? He walked away from the real, final full stop.

The River Naver, Scotland

A Norfolk Scene

Poppies, cow parsley and a carpet of corn bends down to the flint walled village. The church tower still shines a lamp at night, acting as a light house to the ships offshore, warning them of the sand banks and the swift currents that flow there.

But in winter, the church light is one of the few that shows. Most of the cottages are second homes or have been bought up by time share companies. The village pub, shop and garage have gone, starved of custom after October. The bus no longer calls at the village school, closed and belonging to an American executive. The old quayside silted over the years and local fishermen were forced away. The farmer who employed thirty men now makes his profit with three and chemical fertilizer. He hopes to sell the cornfield off as a golf course, the perfect compliment to the marina planned for the creek and bay.

This is how grossly a painting can flatter and gloss over the cruellest of countryside changes.

A Norfolk Scene

The Creek

During the day, the creek perspires under the sun with the merest backbone of water trickling down it. The boats lie in the mud and the little green crabs hide under the weed and damp stones. Terns pick around in the ooze and the skylarks sing over the marsh. A village girl walks along the path on her way to pick samphire - the short sea asparagus - and meets her two neighbours returning with a sack of cockles. And, apart from one other man sitting in the shade of a hull mending a crab pot, that is all the daytime life of the creek.

Towards evening, however, the tide turns, covers the mudflats, lifts the boats and has them tugging at their moorings. A procession of dusty vehicles bumps its way down the track to the staithe. Within fifteen minutes, dinghies are sailing in the sea lagoon and a little boat is under way for a couple of days fishing the bass, skate and mackerel of the Wash. There go a father and son rowing out to handline for a feed of dabs and one boat hopes to net a shoal of creek mullet.

But now the shadows are long and the moon begins to rise. Sails are lowered, fish are laid out and the water begins to suck and gurgle its way back to the sea.

Thornham Creek, Norfolk

All paintings are the copyright of Shirley Deterding.

Appendix - Artist's Note

Shirley is best known as an oil painter. She generally uses canvas but when travelling abroad or back packing in the wilds she will paint on prepared board in a specifically designed carrying box. Otherwise she uses watercolours for capturing the fleeting images of wildlife and water on the move. Shirley does not like using acrylic because the colours tend to be rather harsh and she prefers the softness of oil and watercolour. The freshness of her work is due to the fact that she paints on site, in all weathers. Hazards abound and she has beaten many a retreat from the Scottish midges and even an Alaskan brown bear.

She would like to thank the many people who have commissioned her paintings and the many friends she has made through her work. Her particular thanks go to the following:

Page 18. The Lady of Glencoe. A Poem by Mr. R. Findlay, ghillie, River Dee.

Page 21. Cley Mill, Norfolk - Mr. and Mrs. Nicholas Boldero.

Page 23. The Norfolk Broads - Mr. David Cargill.

Page 25. River Dee, Scotland - Mr. Robert Wright.

Page 27. River Tay, Scotland - Col. W. Bewsher.

Page 29. River Spey, Scotland - Mr. Phillip Paxman.

Page 31. River Dionard, Scotland - Mr Peter Runciman.

Page 35. River Kennett, Hungerford - Mr Tony Duncan.

Page 37. River Dee, Scotland - Baron Charles Burnell-Nugent.

Page 43. River Gruniard, Scotland - Mr Bill Ferguson.

Page 47. Kelling Lake, Norfolk - Mr. and Mrs. Anthony Warin.

Page 51. River Tay, Scotland - Major Ivan Straker.

Page 67. A Norfolk Stillwater - Mr Arthur Haley.

Page 69. River Gruniard, Scotland - Mr Bill Ferguson.

Page 73. River Findhorn, Scotland - Mr Mark Birkbeck.

Page 79. Langa River, Iceland - Mr Alan Mann.

Page 85. The Isle of Mull - Col. W. Bewsher.

Page 89. River Naver, Scotland - Mr. David Midwood.